THE
Quest

THE Quest

*A Journey of Overcoming
Modern-Day Problems Through
Ancient Solutions in Spirituality
Without Religiosity*

Frank Ong

PARTRIDGE

Library of Congress Control Number:		2017944039
ISBN:	Hardcover	978-1-5437-4134-6
	Softcover	978-1-5437-4133-9
	eBook	978-1-5437-4132-2

To order additional copies of this book, contact
Toll Free 800 101 2657 (Singapore)
Toll Free 1 800 81 7340 (Malaysia)
orders.singapore@partridgepublishing.com

www.partridgepublishing.com/singapore

Introduction

Spiritual understanding is essentially divided into two groups: theistic and non-theistic. Theistic is the belief of a creator. Monotheistic Abrahamic religions (i.e., belief in the God of Abraham), such as Judaism, Christianity, and Islam, believe that we are born as sinners and God is the salvation; therefore, one should have faith in God and have him be the centre of one's life.

Non-theistic beliefs pertain to spirituality without religiosity, such as Indian Vedas, Chinese, and Buddhist philosophies. It's about cultivating the innate good in all of us – self-cultivation to handle problems and self-dependence through understanding, practice, and wisdom.

Polytheistic religions like Hinduism or certain Chinese sects are a combination of both. Thus, in this retrospect, it all depends on one's motivation, purpose, discipline, and mental capacity in choosing what suits one most.

Difference between theism and non-theism

Abrahamic religions are often regarded as the religion of one book (i.e., the Torah, Bible, or Al Quran). Salvation can be achieved quite instantly with the acceptance of God as the Saviour or prophet into one's life. Forgiveness of sins is rendered through asking, confession, or repentance. Everyone is born a sinner as an inheritance from the sin of Adam. In times of difficulties and problems, faith in God will overcome it.

In non-theistic beliefs, study, understanding, and practice are the only ways towards self-cultivation. Indian, Buddhist, and Chinese philosophical text are numbered in the thousands, covering every aspect of life. It takes years, decades, or lifetimes of study and practice to achieve "enlightenment". The belief is that everyone is born with an innate good nature as an innocent newborn baby. Such beliefs teach the intrinsic state of the mind, cultivating ourselves, and understanding the causes of suffering and overcoming it.

Not everyone will order or like the same food when eating in a restaurant, but all can share and enjoy eating together on the same table. Nor will all be of one belief or faith, at least not in this lifetime of ours.

Preface

Scott Lee, a successful corporate man, had lived a healthy life but suffered from several bouts of depressions and blockages of coronary heart arteries throughout his twenty-seven-year career.

While recovering from several episodes of depression and having four stents inserted in his heart arteries, he began the search for answers. Despite all the years of watching his diet and exercising, he could not understand what still caused his mental and heart illnesses.

The quest to find an answer was a matter of life and death, as relapse in depression is highly probable and life-threatening. Furthermore, two other blockages in other arteries could expand, causing a high risk of having new blockages or other heart complications.

After reading several books on ancient Eastern philosophies, Scott decided to learn more about it by travelling to Bhutan. It was a journey done alone, without prior experiences, planning, or research about the country's culture and history.

Being a secular person from a Chinese culture background, Lee also immersed himself with ancient Eastern philosophy books, hoping to learn, understand, and practice cultivating mental and physical health naturally.

It was in Bhutan that he learned more about meditation and Buddhist philosophy. Despite it being one of the poorest countries in the world, Bhutan was fascinating because it was also one of the happiest.

The quest for answers then brought him to Thailand, Taiwan, China, Tibet, Northern India, Nepal, and the Himalayas, where he spent time living in various monasteries, temples, and forests without any religious intentions.

With several years of learning, Scott decided to put to test all that he had studied and practiced. He quit all his medications, ate whatever he liked, and even neglected his regular physical exercises, all against his doctor's advice.

Twelve years later, Scott decided to write about his journey, modern daily life, corporate problems, and experiences in overcoming them through ancient wisdoms. The book entailed life's constant struggles, romance, family and corporate life, physical health, and mental well-being.

This is a real-life book about a person's determination in learning about the intrinsic nature of the mind and causes of one's own suffering. This person experienced a decade of learning, reasoning, and practising ancient Eastern philosophical teachings about self-cultivation, prevention, and sustaining mental, physical, and emotional well-being.

The modern world has provided lots of external daily comforts, conveniences, and cures of most illnesses, but it is still in its infant stage of understanding fundamentals of mental health, particularly the mind.

For centuries, ancient philosophers have concentrated on mental well-being by understanding its causes and effects and promoting self-cultivation as well as ways to prevent and overcome it.

This story is about the quest and journey in understanding and overcoming modern problems with ancient solutions.

The Quest

After leaving his job and ending a three-year relationship with a wonderful woman Scott had thought was his soulmate, he again experienced pain in his chest.

Scott was now forty-plus years old. He had had a successful career in the oil trading industry, spanning over two decades. He had two wonderful teenagers, a great career, and a decent pay cheque that provided him and his family with a comfortable lifestyle.

"Your heart arteries have two major blockages, and you will need to undergo an immediate angioplasty procedure," the heart doctor said.

Scott's mind exclaimed, *Not again! Two more major blockages plus two minor ones, despite having stents in two other arteries before.* "Why is this happening again?" he asked his doctor. "I have lived and eaten healthily, plus worked out regularly. How can this be happening again?" His doctor merely replied that it could be due to various reasons, from heredity and lifestyle to stress.

Several years earlier, after an angioplasty for two other blockages, Scott had embarked on a physically disciplined and healthy lifestyle. He ate and drink moderately, stopped late night outings and entertaining, except on special occasions, and exercised regularly. Yet Scott now had to undergo another angioplasty. He was bewildered, worried, and frustrated.

For someone who had almost everything, Scott had also suffered several bouts of severe depression, knowingly and unknowingly. He had now fallen into another depression, an illness common in those experiencing relapses.

Depression may not be physically apparent, but it is mentally and emotionally tormenting. It is often regarded as one of the most mentally suffering illness.

Worry, fear, anxiety, and sadness constantly filled Scott's mind when depressed. He could only see the negativity in almost everything and was incapable of positive thinking for any significant length of time. His body was barely able to perform any important task, while his mind struggled between life and death each day.

Scott stopped living when suffering from depression. Its closest description would be waking up to a nightmare each day, while sleep provided a temporary relief from a mind that had become uncontrollable.

He often considered suicide as his only relief from such mental sufferings. His mind often prompted, just as it learned in ancient teachings, "There is no greater good or harm that a person could do to themselves than from their own mind" (Buddha).

Depression is probably the only illness that causes many physically healthy people to choose to take their lives. Terminally ill people who are mentally positive do not often kill themselves, and they often get better. The photos of Scott's children were both his deterrent from jumping off the building and his inspiration to get well.

"What can I do to get out of it and to prevent this from happening again?" That was the question Scott had for his psychiatrist. Scott knew exactly how tormenting and dangerous depression could be.

The doctor replied, "You could try meditation."

Meditation is commonly known in most parts of Asia, but most urban dwellers, like Scott, know nothing about it. For most, meditation is simply a practice that is advocated in ancient Chinese, Indian, and Buddhist philosophies for an individual's mental cultivation. This is mandatory for monks and nuns, and nonmonastic individuals have practiced it for centuries. There is also the misconception of it being a religious ritual and the emptying of the mind. These could not be further from the truth, as Scott eventually discovered.

Having to take medication for both his heart and depression was expensive and troublesome. Scott had to deal with up to twelve pills each day for years, some for the rest of his life. Psychiatrists often prescribe myriad year-long antidepressants both as a cure and to prevent relapses for most patients. Cardiologists will recommend blood thinners or cholesterol medication for a lifetime to those who have undergone angioplasty.

The Chinese word for heart and mind is *xin*. Written, it is shaped like a heart. That word, along with three arteries, was to become Scott's most crucial discovery in dealing with his heart illness and depression through the wisdom of ancient Eastern teachings. Unlike English, most if not all ancient languages and existing Eastern languages use similar or identical words to describe the heart and mind. This correlation between heart and mind has been taught for centuries. It's been referred to simultaneously and constantly phrased in oneness by ancient Eastern philosophies and existing texts.

In traditional Asian and Chinese families, one points to the chest instead of the head when referring to the mind. The word *xin* was often used when referring to either the heart or the mind. It became Scott's quest to find an alternative way to prevent and overcome his heart and mind illnesses, which was now a matter of life and death.

Scott was raised in a small town called Taiping, in the north peninsula of Malaysia. He excelled in his high school before moving to the capital, Kuala Lumpur, for tertiary education. After graduating, he moved to Singapore in search of a better future. The timing was less than perfect, as Asia was undergoing one of its toughest recessions.

Scott found a job as a hotel receptionist, despite having graduated from a good university in Malaysia. He was also doing part-time tutoring and selling coffee beans for extra income. It was physically and mentally tiring most of the time, but he was young and had only himself to depend on in a new country.

Home was a storage room on the ground floor in an old four-storey walk-up apartment. There was barely enough space for a single mattress plus a small TV cabinet at the end of it. The door had to be opened during the daytime for light to shine into the room. Clothes had to be hung on the walls, and a tiny light bulb hanging from the ceiling was the only source of light during the night. Comfort in the hot and humid room came from a small fan. The old TV had an antenna that needed to be adjusted regularly for better reception, but not without giving off electric shocks.

An elderly Malay divorcee living with her young son and three cats was Scott's neighbour. The smell of her cooking outside her room regularly made him salivate, and she occasionally shared food with him. He reciprocated by buying her some groceries.

Scott did not have much; neither did his neighbour. But both were content with what they had. After all, contentment was being taught to be the greatest wealth in Eastern teachings.

When the economy recovered, Scott found a job at an oil trading company. It was something he was very keen at, and he excelled in it while enjoying the job. It was like the old Chinese saying "If you love what you do, you will never have to work another day" (Confucius). Scott had good relationships with his employer and colleagues, and he worked in a friendly environment. This job eventually turned out to be Scott's entire twenty-seven-year working career, until he retired at the age of fifty.

Going to work was something Scott looked forward to, despite the long commute by foot and bus. Learning on the job was fulfilling and rewarding. It was the chance of a lifetime to become part of one of the biggest industries around and earn top dollar.

In the first few years alone, Scott was promoted several times. He was eventually promoted to a managerial position and given more responsibilities. He travelled more frequently to source and develop new businesses. He was one of the youngest oil traders in this close-knit community and suffered his fair share of intimidation and bullying tactics by much older traders. However, that did not deter him from advancing in this career.

From living sparingly and not having proper meals, Scott was then engaging in sumptuous business meals and golf games as part of the entertaining culture in this industry. It was a life-changer for this young man from a small town who had only twenty Singapore dollars when he came to Singapore. By then, he was seeing an ex-colleague from the hotel, and after a brief courtship, they decided to settle down and start a family.

Through living simply in the small storage room over the years, Scott had managed to save a considerable sum, which, with some help from his wife's savings, would partly pay for a new home. It was a cosy two-bedroom apartment surrounded by greeneries in a garden-like atmosphere, appropriately named The Dairy Farm.

A year later, they were blessed with the arrival of a son, who was born a couple of months premature. His chances of survival were very low due to his underdeveloped body. Without proper insurance and paternity medical benefits, Scott had to use almost his entire savings for his son's month-long hospitalization. Fortunately, he grew big enough to be taken out of the intensive care unit and be handled like a normal baby.

Scott's wife had to leave her job to take care of the child, leaving him to be the only breadwinner for the young family. As with most couples living in a cosmopolitan city, having dual incomes was crucial to sustaining a home and providing for a family. The extra income from Scott's wife would help, but they decided it was best to raise the child themselves rather than through a domestic helper, which was rather common in this part of the world.

Two years later, they had a daughter; she was born after the full pregnancy term, unlike her older brother.

With a growing family, ageing parents and in laws, Scott's financial commitment increased exponentially.

He had grown up in a similar situation, like his father, who was the only breadwinner in the family. His dad had also been a prudent man who wore the same slippers and clothes for years, as long as they were still wearable. He had never taken a holiday from his business, and he wouldn't spend anything on himself.

As with his dad, all Scott's family needed was financial discipline, such as cutting down on social events like eating out, shopping, or holidaying, to spend within their means and not live on credit. Despite being prudent, Scott's family were living comfortably.

However, during Scott's childhood, his relationship with his father was cold, unlike the warmth experienced by his siblings and his father. He was a rebellious teenager and a non-conformist, while his father was a traditional conservative Chinese businessperson who, at a very young age, had migrated to Malaysia during the Cultural Revolution in China.

They were constantly at each other's throats in all that they did, and Scott's mother often had to be the peacemaker to prevent situations from escalating. However, the relationship would turn into one that was respecting and warm when his father fell ill during his last few years of life.

After seven years, Scott was approached by an ex–business counterpart to jointly work for him and several Indonesian shareholders in another company; he had seen Scott excelling in what he did during all those years. Things seem to flow nicely, but then Scott's father became gravely ill and had to be hospitalised in hospitals located in several bigger cities. Scott had to travel back and forth to visit, which was a ten-hour drive, taking his father in and out of hospitals for a few years, sharing these responsibilities with his younger siblings, but also having to focus on his work and family.

At work, things started to fall apart after a few years; it became a daily moral struggle. Profits were prioritised over ethics; morality was secondary; and his employer's greed was insatiable. Scott had successfully brought in significant profits year after year, but as Gandhi once said, "The world has enough to satisfy the need of everyone but not the greed of one person." It was never ever enough for the company.

The last straw was when he had to choose between morality and ethics or pleasing his bosses further. Scott subsequently had to leave the company for sticking up with his moral principles instead of giving in to his employer's greed in order to protect his job.

It became a financially trying time for the only breadwinner. He had to provide for his young family, pay the mortgage for their home, and take care of his father's medical expenses. Being the eldest son in an Asian family, Scott had to fulfil most financial obligations, as his younger siblings were just starting out in their respective careers. Scott was depressed but had to keep his parents in the dark about his unemployment.

His father eventually succumbed to his illness several months later. It was a devastating moment for Scott, who, as mentioned, had just recently developed a close relationship with his father after all these years. While keeping his unemployment a secret from his mother, siblings, and relatives, Scott had to put on a brave face during financial uncertainty.

A few months later, Scott had to sell his matrimonial home and rent a modest apartment for his family to ensure he had enough funds to provide for them if his unemployment dragged on for a long period.

Moving from a small but comfortable private apartment with all the recreational facilities in a private resort-like property to living amongst foreign blue-collar workers took a while to get used to. Scott's children were too young to know the difference, but Scott and his wife had lived a simple life in the past.

Constant sadness and worries from dealing with his father's death, providing for his young family, and uncertainty about getting a new job turned each waking hour into nightmare for Scott.

His thoughts were filled with regret about how he had not appreciated his father more in the past as well as his worries about the future. The worries turned into fear, and fear turned into anxiety.

Scott's mental health began to deteriorate further as days and nights passed. Either he would sleep the entire day or he couldn't sleep at all. Seeing his young children gave him comfort but also brought tears to his eyes at the same time, as love and anxiety were often bundled into a single emotion.

Scott had enough in savings to last for a couple of years, but negative thoughts exaggerated his problems into self-projected desperation. What if he could not find another job soon? What would happen to his children if his savings ran out? Where would they live?

If only he had known at that time of a profound ancient quote not to dwell in the past, as it consists of just memories or worry about the future, as it is just imagination … One needs to live in the present, which is the reality. Scott would have been in a better state of mind.

In ancient Eastern teachings, ignorance is regarded as the cause of one's sufferings, along with greed, desire and attachment as well as anger, hatred and aversion.

Scott twice struggled with these emotional traumas for months, first when he left his job and later when his father died. To him, it was just a part of life. However, the Eastern ancients also stated that nothing good lasts; nothing bad lasts either. All things are impermanent.

Unexpectedly, a Japanese friend who had dealt with Scott for many years approached and offered him a position in the company he was heading. Scott knew this company well and had dealt closely with them for years. His new colleagues were people he had known as former business partners. Despite being a new employee there, Scott was neither a stranger nor felt like an outsider in the new organisation. It was an organisation filled with hard-working people, which is the trademark of Japanese employees, who are typically helpful towards one another.

Scott's latest salary was much lower than before, but he was happier there than in his previous environment. One of Scott's main responsibilities was to change the company from the typical Japanese corporate system into one with an international mindset.

It was an enormous task, but Scott found it more fulfilling. Changing Japanese centuries-old way of mentality in dealing with their company was almost an impossible task, as Scott found out in later years. However, in just a span of a few years, Scott was promoted to senior management. It was not the norm for a Japanese company to have a non-Japanese in such a position. Unlike Western companies, many

Eastern companies are less liberal in providing equal opportunities for outsiders.

Scott was focussed on the task he was hired for, but going against superiors in a Japanese company is one of the most offensive things one can do. Being unfamiliar with their culture, Scott pushed for more reform and was partially successful in his objective to streamline the company internationally. For the first time, non-Japanese staff members were then given the same opportunities as their Japanese counterparts.

By then, Scott had saved enough despite earning less, and with that income, after staying in the public rented apartment for years, he bought a new private home for his family. But in view of his workload and late nights, he and his wife continued to sleep in separate rooms, just as they started doing after having their second child.

Their pre-marriage courtship had been brief and sweet, but constant late night working hours, travelling, and overseas assignments drifted them apart. Living in separate rooms started out for practical reasons due to work and raising two young kids in a small two-bedroom apartment. As the years passed, Scott and his wife were no longer able to engage physically as a normal husband and wife. Romance no longer existed, but the caring, respect for one another, and responsibilities of being parents were always present.

Scott was then transferred to California to develop new businesses. San Francisco offered Scott a change of environment and wider experiences. Travelling regularly across the United States was often tiring but was also a revelation. Scott was now being influenced by the Western social and corporate lifestyle. Individualism is pretty much a way of life there. Voicing opposing opinions is acceptable in Western corporate culture, and emotions are often released instead of being controlled or contained.

Scott returned to Singapore after his assignment, but now ego, anger, and pride often got the best of him. Despite being good at what he did, his temperament was his biggest nemesis. Instead of being tolerant and controlling his emotions, as most ancient Eastern teachings advocate, Scott's idea of dealing with dissatisfactions was to let them out and to speak out anytime he disagreed with something. He became his worst enemy.

An angry person is often said to be almost insane, justifying further the term for one to not lose his mind. In times of anger, Scott would often exaggerate something that his colleagues had done or said incorrectly, forgetting all the help that they had provided for him previously. The tendency of an angry person is to focus, exaggerate, and expound on the mistakes another person has made, while ignoring all the good rendered to him by this same individual in the past.

Anger is regarded as one of the most destructive emotions, both mentally and physically, and per Buddha, holding on to our anger is tantamount to holding on to a hot coal with the intention of throwing it at someone. We are the ones who get hurt.

Without realising the harm that he was doing to himself, Scott had thought that emotions should not be kept inside but released so they would not get blown up. This mindset contradicts ancient wisdoms that constantly advocate self-control to avoid having to face the consequences of anger: "When anger rises, think of its consequences" (Lao Tzu).

Another of Lao Tzu's quotes: "To be patient in a moment of anger is said to avoid a hundred days of sorrows."

To achieve that, as advised by Confucius himself, is to not make any remarks when angry and not make any promises when happy. Decisions that are made under the influence of emotions often garner negative results. It is only when one is calm and composed that decisions can be made logically and sensibly.

Yet Scott was often speaking his mind, especially so when his subordinates were not treating him in a way that he considered fairly or when his superiors were not supporting him. This did not go over well with his Japanese colleagues, but unlike Scott, they had always been taught to keep emotions inside. In fact, the Japanese way of disagreeing is with silence. They were most tolerant of him.

Fortunately, most agreed with what he said, but not necessarily the way he said it, as none that was being said was for Scott's own vested interest. But going against fellow Japanese in support of their foreign colleague is unacceptable in this deep-rooted culture. Scott had not realised how closely knitted Japanese corporate communities had always been.

As with most multinational companies, job rotation was the norm. The old management that had brought

Scott over to reform the company was now being transferred to other departments and was substituted by a new team.

The new management's intention was simply to go back to running it the traditional Japanese way, and for Scott it was years of work going down the drain. The amicable, warm working relationship with former colleagues conflicted with the cold treatment he received from new ones. He continued to stick it out with the company, but just as a wise sage said, "The best strokes of luck are often not getting what we want."

Scott was approached by the owner of a company looking for immediate expansion. He had a most generous offer. He offered Scott a lucrative contract due to his wide experiences, which would provide him with a living that most would envy. He was given a country club membership, chauffeur-driven car, a nice office, and various other generous benefits in addition to the much better pay package.

Being a newcomer with a most senior position, Scott had to encounter office politics of envy and jealousy from pioneer staffs in this company, both in higher and lower positions, almost immediately. The owner who had hired him stayed overseas, taking care of his other businesses, and was not around most of the time.

Again, Scott was regarded as an intruding outsider almost as soon as he was being hired. The generous package and change of management in his old company were his consoling factors, plus the hope that things would be better in the future with this new one.

Despite being a temperamental person, Scott, having been raised in a conservative Chinese family, had always been exposed to good virtues. As with many profit-orientated companies, profits coupled with office politics of backstabbing and envy are a part of many corporate lives, but unlike Scott's previous Japanese company, helping one another was not part of this new company culture.

Being in a senior position required him to deal with lots of pressure from having to make money constantly, dealing with his colleagues, and regular travelling. While this provided him with an exceptionally comfortable lifestyle and lots of material things, it didn't give him sustainable satisfaction or happiness.

Having an unhealthy working environment affected him mentally, despite all its privileges. A bigger home and luxury cars provided more comfort for the family, but they did not benefit Scott's mental and physical well-being.

This was then when he experienced pain in his chest and discovered that two of his heart arteries were blocked. He had to immediately undergo his first angioplasty to insert stents into the blocked arteries to unclog them, but he returned to work almost immediately.

That changed Scott's lifestyle. Exercising became a regular routine, he quit smoking, and eating healthily soon followed. That was what he thought was needed to prevent any recurrences and to develop a healthy heart.

While he had all the material comforts, there wasn't any romance, as Scott and his wife had not had any physical contact as husband and wife for more than a decade. What he thought he needed to be truly happy was a new romance and companionship.

However, as his children were still young, Scott and his wife decided to stay together for their sake, despite not being able to be physically engaged like any normal couples. Scott and his wife had annual family trips and holidays with the kids, but never as a couple alone.

Scott's two children soon became mature teenagers; they were incredibly brilliant and well behaved. His wife was supportive of his work but agreed that both could now live out their own lives as they chose. Scott would nevertheless continue to provide for all their financial and material needs.

Terms for divorce were discussed amicably, but both agreed that unless one decided to remarry, it was not an urgent matter to pursue for the time being for the sake of their children. As spouses, they were only good friends, but they always remained dedicated parents to their kids.

Eventually, Scott moved out of the family home to stay on his own. He lived alone for several years, first in a rented apartment, and then he bought a new one, never neglecting his obligation to provide the best for his family and perform his fatherly duty to his kids.

He maintained regular trice weekly visits to his home, spending time with his kids and his now-separated wife during meals. Having his own freedom was what he felt he needed to enjoy more of a social life.

In between working, travelling, and entertaining, Scott embarked on investing in several entertainment and food and beverage businesses. Attending social gatherings in his business outlets and making new friends were part of his new life. He was on the right track – or at least that's what he thought. He had everything a man could ask for, plus more.

To him, happiness was having fancy cars, expensive watches, and clothes, but none of this so-called happiness lasted for long. It wasn't long before Scott met a kind, sincere, and gorgeous woman. He told her of his marital and family situation but asked that she be patient for a few years, until his kids were older. She understood his situation and was willing to wait.

At first, the relationship was platonic, with mutual respect. Scott's companion was extremely attractive, kind, and supportive. As months passed, the romance flourished.

Being in love was what Scott had hoped to experience again, and he had believed it was the missing link to complete the circle of his life. He assumed that good companionship was all he needed and that she was to be the source of his happiness.

Like most, Scott was seeking happiness from others in thinking that his own happiness could be provided from a loved one, which is contrary with old wisdom teachings that happiness is dependent solely on oneself or is an inside job.

Scott was confident that she was the person that he would want to spend his life with, and for him it was the second chance at romance. As for her, marriage and raising a family were what she had wished for years, and time was running out, as she was in her late thirties.

They both prioritised their time for each other, as most new couples do, and their romance grew deeper. In times like this, all one sees is the bright side of the other while trying to be the shining one at the same time. But as the emotions grow, often so do the attachments towards each other – attachments which gradually morph into dependency and develop into a sense of ownership between both parties. Emotions often take precedence over logic, and romance would seem to be able to last forever, just as in the love stories, with their common ending of living happily ever after.

They tried to spend as much time together as possible, despite their busy schedules. Weeks or months of overseas assignments required them to be temporarily separated. Meeting in different parts of the world was the only way to fill the gaps of long absence.

Scott enjoyed the companionship, and he was making new friends from social outings with his companion. For the first time in almost two decades, he could do things as part of a couple again. Whatever brief opportunities there were, they spent watching movies, dining, and travelling together, something Scott and his separated wife hasn't done much of during their courtship and done none at all after marriage.

However, despite fulfilling what conventional romance had prescribed, Scott could not find sustainable peace of mind. He was either constantly trying to please her, feeling concerned about not doing enough, or fearing losing her. Would he be able to provide the best for her, to make her happy? Was he good enough for her? These were the spiral of constant questions in his mind.

For Scott, as the attachment grew deeper, the more troubling those questions became, and the guilt of leaving his kids and their mother began reliving in him. He was torn between being selfish in living out his own life and the obligation of living his life with his children as a responsible father.

This guilt of not being around his kids was constantly filling his mind, despite having frequent contact and visits with the blessings from both his separated wife and companion.

He began to wonder what had prevented him from having peace of mind when all things seemed to be going well. Was it that he felt guilty about not living with his family in their home? Or was it due to more work pressure from having a bigger responsibility and having to make even more money to gain the favour of his office colleagues?

As he went back regularly for dinner with his kids, he would often ask if they would prefer him to move back. Surprisingly, his kids and wife preferred him to stay on his own and live his own life, either alone or with whomever he chose to be. This might have been due to they being happier without him around, not having to deal with his temperament, or just wanting Scott to be a happier person.

With these unstoppable thoughts, Scott was again mentally and emotionally down not long after moving out from his home. This time, though, he researched depressive mood and decided to seek an early treatment from a psychiatrist to prevent it. However, once his mind was in control over him, he couldn't do much anymore.

The choice of choosing to live with his companion over his children was constantly a no-win situation battle going through his head. From that, anxiety and fear soon developed. Scott had hope that this would be just a temporary emotional setback, but as weeks passed without any improvement, he figured he had to seek professional help.

He was diagnosed as suffering from depression and was prescribed several months of medication. Scott kept this from his employer thinking he could overcome it with medication. Unfortunately, antidepressants often come with many side effects. Drowsiness was one that Scott had to bear during office hours. It was a very difficult period for him, both mentally and physically.

Scott's supportive companion stood by him during his depression. However, the closest ones are often affected the most, both emotionally and mentally, from a depressed person. Scott appreciated the understanding, comfort, and perseverance of his companion during those few difficult months and felt more confident of their relationship.

Scott eventually recovered after a year of medication, and he continued to live on his own. His wonderful companion was his soul mate; his kids were doing well in school and all their needs were well taken care of and provided for. It was having the best of both worlds. However, such a perfect world cannot last. As the old saying goes, nothing is permanent.

These issues, including having to consider divorce soon to marry his companion, the possibility of seeing less of his children, and worrying how it would affect them, would again take their toll in the years to come.

Scott stayed on for four years to finish his contract. Despite bringing in record profits for his company during this duration, he could not win his lone battle against longer serving colleagues working together to oust him. As with hyenas scavenging for a kill after grabbing it from another predator, they eventually fought amongst themselves for both the financial and material benefits that were once being provided for Scott.

To make matters worse, his companion decided to leave him for the sake of morality. As the principled person she was, she felt she had waited long enough. She felt it wasn't right to be with him since he was still not legally divorced and time was not on her side to raise a family. Age was catching up, as was the uncertainty of Scott's having a future with her.

His dreamlike world was now a nightmare. With no job to keep him occupied and losing the perfect companion that he had hoped to be with for life was too much for him to handle on his own. He tried his best to get back to her, but as his approaches were not reciprocated, hope turned into frustration. Scott was a complete emotionally wrecked person. Like many, he tried to find escapism from his mental torments through drinking. While this may have made him emotionally numb for the night, it always aggravated his mental state the next day.

In Scott's head, everything seemed hopeless and negative thoughts were piling over one another until they became both uncontrollable and fearful. Often he wished that a comet or a huge natural disaster would just destroy the world. For those who have experienced depression, Armageddon is often seen as the better alternative over the guilt of suicide. The constant praying for even temporary peace of mind is a cry for help when one is constantly filled with negativities and the trauma of self-projected crisis situations.

It's common for many to feel sad or worry all the time, but when these feelings, coupled with anxiety and fear, continue for several weeks, it's a sign of looming depression. Scott knew this all too well, and despite reminding himself of all the motivational quotes he had in his library of self-help books, none could calm his mind. He had to cultivate his mental health through practice, not just in theory.

Scott then fell into another deeper depression. The doctor who had treated him before told him his level of depression was now at the scale of ten out of ten, which is the highest. Anything above this may cause schizophrenia or, worse still, suicide.

In psychiatry, the severity of depression is measured by the answers given by a patient through a series of questions. The intensity of the level of depression is based from the ascending scale from one to ten, with ten being most severe. Anything above this may reflect schizophrenia, which is a medical term for an unsound mind that involves the hearing of voices.

As previous long-term medication had failed to prevent relapses into depression, Scott decided to study meditation as the practical means to achieve peace of mind. After months of studying, Scott went for meditation classes taught by Buddhist monks. It seemed to calm his mind a bit. That was his first experience in meditation.

That small dose of mental calmness while meditating was the stepping stone for Scott to learn and practice more. This was also the end of drinking bouts, but Scott was now again on another long-term treatment of antidepressants and had to deal with constant various side effects ranging from overeating and sleeping as well as urinary complications.

For Scott, this was a personal insight and experience into an ancient wisdom that had been taught and practised for centuries. Meditation is simply the training of the mind to tame and calm it from the nonstop flow of thoughts by diverting the awareness to the observation of one's breath.

Simply counting the breaths from one to ten without any thoughts is a monumental task even for normal people, despite how simplistic it may sound, and it is impossible for those who are in depression. This shows how busy the mind is all the time, even while sleeping, when the subtler mind is in action during dreams.

Like many, Scott had his own misconception of meditation being a religious practice or keeping the mind empty. Using the breath as a tool to divert the attention from other thoughts is the most natural thing to do, and it's completely secular. Similarly, in many other ancient exercises, such as tai chi, qigong, and yoga, the breath is being used to connect the body and mind.

Scott now realised that to be fully in control of his life, he must learn to tame his mind and take control of it instead of letting it wander off wildly. Ancient quotes teach the following: "Those who control their minds control their lives" (Buddha) and "If you correct your mind, the rest of your life will fall into place" (Lao Tzu).

There are generally two types of meditation: mindfulness (*samatha*) and analytical (*vipassana*). These are contemplative meditations.

1) Calm abiding meditation mindfulness: to calm the mind by focusing on the breath. In other words, it is the prolonging of the gap in between thoughts which we often experience unknowingly for a brief moment.

2) Analytical meditation – mindfulness and analytical: to be aware of the breath while analysing the intrinsic state of the mind and body and experiencing the nature of phenomena. It is also a prerequisite to the understanding and reasoning of profound ancient's teachings through deep contemplation.

These Sanskrit terms that are commonly used in Theravada Buddhism are more common in South Asia. Meditation is divided into these ways to calm the mind and cultivate wisdom through analysing and reasoning.

In summary, meditation is the penetration through the clouds (which are thoughts) to a clear sky or the penetration beneath the ocean, where it's calm, from the volatile waves of thoughts on its surface. For is it said that the intrinsic nature of the mind is clarity and calmness, which has been taught since ancient times; and wisdom is essential to understand the impermanence of thoughts.

Scott began to study more, particularly ancient Chinese and Buddhist philosophies about cultivating and developing mental health. He was not a religious person, nor did he intend to be one. Coincidently, all that he studied involved logical reasoning philosophy. However, a couple of months later, he felt some tightness in his chest and went for a full checkup.

"Your heart arteries have two major blockages, and you will need to undergo an immediate angioplasty," the heart doctor said.

Scott's mind exclaimed, *Not again! Two more major blockage plus two other minor ones despite having stents in two other arteries before?*

"Why is this happening again?" he asked his doctor. "I have lived and eaten healthily, plus worked out regularly. How can this be happening?" His doctor merely replied that it could be due to various reasons, from heredity to lifestyle and stresses.

Several years ago, after an earlier angioplasty for two other blockages, Scott had embarked on a physically disciplined and healthy lifestyle. He quit smoking, drank moderately (only on special occasions), and stopped late nights partying and entertaining. Scott underwent the angioplasty procedure again but was left bewildered, worried, and frustrated.

Being alone without a job in a big apartment without anyone to talk to made each day seem longer. Scott began to take long drives in one of his sports car to clear his mind; however, they provided only temporary relief. He began to socialise again, hoping to fill the gaps of each seemingly long day. However, Scott was in no mental or emotional position to be involved with anyone. Going back home to be with his children was the only time he looked forward to, and returning to his own apartment had slowly become traumatic. Scott then buried himself with more ancient Chinese and Buddhist philosophical books.

All the material things that Scott had once thought to be his source of happiness had slowly become a burden. Cars needed to be serviced and maintained regularly, furniture had to be cleaned, and mortgages of his homes were beginning to drain his savings and contribute to more mental stress.

While Scott was not in any immediate danger of running out of funds, it was nevertheless a psychological financial warfare evolving in his head. The only time Scott's mind was calmer was when he meditated. As days and weeks passed, Scott's mental health seemed to stabilise rather than deteriorate further.

"What you think, you become" and "All that we think, say, or do is nothing but reflections of our thoughts" were some of the ancient quotes Scott had learned, memorized, and constantly reminded himself of.

It turns out that these were in fact Scott's discovery as to the cause of his depression. He was being controlled by his mind rather than having control over it. It has been running freely and wild for ages, with thoughts after thoughts, from the time he woke up until he slept. Small problems were often exaggerated into big ones.

The future seems so bleak and dark in a depressed person's mind. Suicide seem like the only sensible way out, the only relief from such tremendous mental sufferings.

Meditation was now his way of putting the theories from all he had learned into practice, to test and experience its effectiveness in calming the mind. These practices were under the guidance of Tibetan and Thai Buddhist monks in the preliminary stages.

It was Scott's personal experience with calmness during meditation that became his conviction to study and further practice what ancient Eastern philosophies had taught for centuries, without any religiosity. The more he read, the further it strengthened his conviction, and with that he became more disciplined in his practice.

It is also said by the ancients that only when we can be convinced ourselves can we be disciplined in practicing anything sustainably. We are our best instructors. The ancient Buddhist quotes that struck Scott most were Buddha's own final words: "Do not accept all that I have taught out of reverence to me but test them out like a goldsmith testing the purity of gold." It's a call to analyse, test, and reason out everything instead of blind faith. Similarly, Chinese ancient philosophical teachings are based on logical thinking.

These ancient teachings resonate with Scott's character of reasoning with logic and the avoidance of blind faith in his professional, social, and personal life. Having been exposed religiously at a very young age, Scott could never find the answers to many of life's problems, such as why children die or why are people are born with deformities and destitution, while others are born with beauty and luxuries. The notion of having a blind faith towards what had happened, what was happening, and what was going to happen could never seem to satisfy his curiosity.

The ancient Eastern philosophy advocates analysing, reasoning, and investigating to acquire the wisdom in understanding the causes of things and dealing with problems but cautions against blind acceptance of anything out of reverence or in faith. This was instrumental in fuelling his passion towards learning it more deeply.

That quote from the Buddha to analyse, reason, and to test his own teachings seemed unorthodox but at the same time advocated using human intelligence and the ability to reason. He had always been a pragmatic person in dealing with life questions. Reasoning was part of his job to convince others, and logic was his foundation in decision-making.

This was to be Scott's journey to recovery from his depression and the beginning of his decade-long quest to deal with modern problems through ancient solutions.

Scott's first direct experience in temporary calming his mind through meditation was a milestone in the self-effort to gain a temporary peace of mind beyond modern medication. Antidepressants are often sedative and function to calm the mind by numbing it.

In certain aspects, such experiences are like getting drunk with alcohol or high with drugs, but with very different motivations and consequences. For a person who is already severely depressed, self-cultivation to cure oneself without medication will be futile, as with most other illnesses. Once the mind has been left to take control over a person, it's an uphill task to overcome it personally, without medical assistance.

The ancient Buddhist quote of "The mind is everything and what you think you become," which Scott had come across many times, reflects well with the state of his depression; and "Those who control their minds control their lives" indicates that he has to overcome this self-induced mental trauma by himself.

Scott had tried exercising, socialising, and getting advice from friends, but none proved to have had any significant lasting effects. The only "exercise" that had proved to be effective was the mental exercise through meditation, which is both internal and self-dependant.

More importantly, Scott is now learning the methods to cultivate and develop his mental health and strength. Because this is an internal struggle, the only way to overcome it should also be done internally.

From a young age, Scott had learned to be self-dependent, and it was time for him to rely on himself again to overcome this mental warfare.

Another ancient philosophical quote that came to his mind: "It is better to conquer ourselves than to win a thousand battles." This reflects the difficulty of self-cultivation and control.

Unlike religion, where one usually bases one's faith in God to overcome problems and predicaments, Eastern philosophical teachings advocate for one to learn to solve one's own problems. This is done through cultivating mental and emotional strength to handle difficult circumstances, understanding the causes and effects of situations as to gain wisdom, and developing perseverance and endurance in overcoming suffering. Self-cultivation requires lots of learning and practicing that involves having the right thoughts, speech, and action in one's daily life.

The only other alternative that Scott had was to rely on antidepressants and to succumb to their unpredictable side effects and risk of addiction. The ancient practice of meditation seemed to be the most natural way in the prevention, cultivation, and development of mental health and was worth his exploring it in greater depths.

Bhutan was Scott's first destination into learning and experiencing more about ancient Eastern philosophy in an ancient country. He was keen to find out how such a poor country was constantly being defined as the happiest country in the world.

He had no knowledge about the country but that it had often been termed the last Shangri-La by some travellers offering the mystical notion towards it. As one of the places to visit on his bucket list, it seemed to be a sensible choice in killing two birds with one stone.

Scott travelled to Bhutan alone, without doing much research or having any prior experiences of being there before. He spent his time in Bhutan doing some trekking, visiting some of its famous landmarks, particularly the monasteries and its national library.

In Bhutan, gross happiness index (GHI) was used to measure the country's well-being rather that gross domestic products used in most countries to measure respective economies. Despite living in a very poor country, Bhutanese seem so much happier and smile more.

The wordings on the wall of the Bhutan National Library remained clearly in his mind: "Anger never ceases with anger but only through loving kindness, this is the natural law." Anger had always been detrimental to Scott's relationship with those around him. The conventional delusion towards the demonstration of anger as a sign of strength could not be further from the truth based on ancient teachings. "He who angers you conquers you," from (Lao Tzu), reflects precisely the opposite

Scott spent a considerable amount of time talking with lamas about Buddhist philosophies, both with the intention of learning and practicing more meditation. This was his first visit to centuries-old monasteries, and it was his first time witnessing and experiencing a Bhutanese monastic life. He spent several weeks there, learning Buddhist philosophy and practicing meditation.

Scott was motivated by the affirmation to the values of ancient Buddhist teachings and the benefits of meditation by various renowned Bhutanese Buddhist monks. It was a trip filled with the splendour of Bhutanese natural beauty, but the teachings that Scott could take home with him was the true value of his trip. This was a journey of knowledge and experience that would be his catalyst for his future travels towards his quest of learning ancient wisdoms.

His anger was the main cause of his mental sufferings for ages and had been detrimental to his physical health. Scott had begun to realise the correlation between mental and physical health.

His previous unhealthy working relationship with his former colleagues and bosses had developed into anger and hatred. The betrayals and backstabbing were constantly playing at the back of his mind. Scott's occasionally fiery outburst of temper was his biggest nemesis. This resonated well, with another quote that says, "You will not be punished for your anger; you will be punished by your anger."

Along with most of Scott's other setback was his greed for more money. Although it never compromised his principle to gain it ethically, his ignorance of finding his happiness through others and the pleasures from material things were always short-lived and often turned into misery.

Greed is the main source of mental vexations, sufferings, and discontentment, as depicted in many ancient teachings. However, with more in-depth study, it also incorporates desire and craving. The fact that it is insatiable is well known and experienced by many. However, the dangers that come with it are often overlooked because of ignorance.

Ancient teachings have also taught that hatred and ignorance are the other main causes of suffering. Scott realised the danger and harm of various negative emotions also being the causes of his own sufferings.

Hatred in ancient literature also incorporates anger and aversion. Unfortunately, most ancient words could not be fully translated into single English vocabularies without being lost in translation but can be more accurately described with several similarities.

Theory without practice wouldn't benefit Scott mentally. He needed to spend some time in several monasteries learning meditation and discussing with lamas about life's sufferings, their causes, and ways to prevent them.

Chiangmai Thailand

Wat Umong Chiangmai

Chiangrai Thailand

Chiangrai Thailand

Bali Indonesia

Mae Salong Thailand

Dharamsala India

Taiping Malaysia

Taroko Taiwan

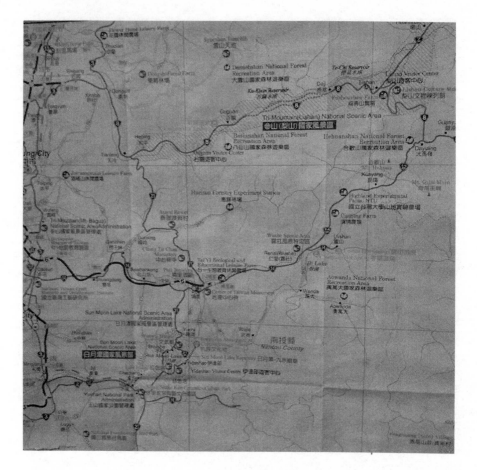

Map

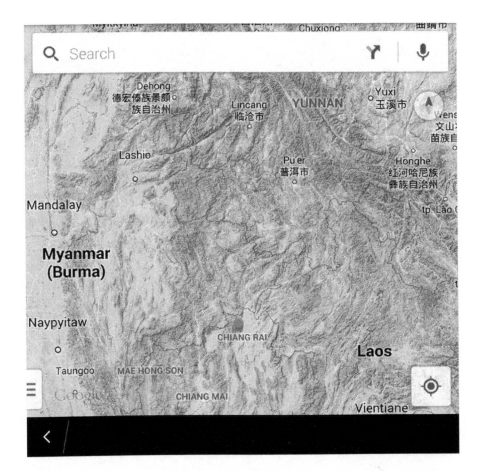

Map

Luang Prabang Laos

Shangri La China

Taiping Home

Lake Gardens Taiping

Lake Gardens Taiping

Lake Gardens Taiping

Saint George Institution Taiping

Taiping Hills

Himalayas

The experiences in Bhutan became the motivation for Scott to travel regularly to Thailand to learn and practice additional ancient Buddhist philosophy and meditation by living in forest temples up in Chiang Mai, situated in North Thailand.

In Chiang Mai, Scott stayed in a famous forest temple called Wat Umong. *Wat* is the Thai word for temple. This is a traditional Buddhist forest temple similar to what was around centuries ago in India. It welcomes guests of any faith or with none to stay there and is one of the few in Thailand that has English-speaking monks.

Accommodation is a basic tiny room with a few old mattresses sprawled on the floor. There is a small ceiling fan, but as it is located in a forest, rooms are often crawling with insects and ants. Buddhist religion prohibits the killing of any animals or insects.

Realising this from his years of studies about Buddhist philosophy, Scott tried to avoid stepping on any of them, seeing them instead as his companions. After all, it was he who had intruded into their "home".

There are no rental fees, and visitors are welcome to stay for up to several weeks. However, it's customary to make a small donation to the temple at the end of the stay.

There are strict rules and regulation to be adhered to while staying or visiting a temple – surprisingly, being Buddhist is not one of them. Dwellers must dress in white clothes, which they can bring themselves or purchase from the temple. No cohabiting with the opposite or same sex is allowed.

Waking time is at 4.30 a.m., and by 5.00 a.m., dwellers are encouraged to practice meditation that the monks taught the day before. This can be in a form of walking or the traditional sitting meditation posture.

At 6.00 a.m., while the monks go off for their collection of food alms in nearby villages, dwellers work together in cleaning up parts of the temple ground, clearing it of the leaves that fills the temple's ground daily and in their respective accommodations, with their best effort to not harm or kill any of the insects.

Breakfast is at 7.00 a.m. and is normally provided by nearby villagers and volunteers cooking in the temples.

Simple plain dishes plus a cup of coffee or tea is all there is to it. Breakfast should only be taken together with monks, after they are back from collecting their alms, and it is eaten in complete silence.

This is also where Scott had learned the benefit of eating consciously, slowly, and in complete silence. A Chinese saying came to his mind: "Everyone eats and drinks, but few know the taste of the food." Whereas in Buddhist philosophy, eating should be done mindfully and moderately.

The benefits of eating this way are the food tastes much better, lesser amount is needed to feel the same fullness, and chewing a lot helps to do most of the work for the digestive system. What Scott had studied in books is now being put into practice.

After breakfast and the cleaning up, it's then a moment for a short relaxation before more meditation practices. Same goes with lunch, with is served before noon, as Theravada Buddhist monks do not eat after midday.

The rest of the day is spent mostly in self-meditation, with occasional relaxation time. No dinner is provided, but dwellers are often encouraged to drink hot drinks to relieve themselves of hunger pangs or to fulfil their stomach. In the night, the monks will then conduct Buddhist teachings or dharma classes for those interested, but they never impose their views on anyone or use them to demote other faiths – nor do they advocate for those attending to adopt them.

Interestingly enough, Buddhism is one of the least self-advocating religions around, encouraging that its entire teaching not be accepted blindly but be thoroughly tested and reasoned out.

What Scott eventually found out from his studies about the way of eating in temples is that this promotes both self-discipline and moderate eating, as Buddhism teaches.

However, in view of different climates, cultures, and practicality, there are different variation and practices adopted by Buddhist monks from different countries in terms of types of food to be eaten, the frequency, and how they are to be obtained.

Thailand is typically hot and humid, with lush forests in suburban areas. Its population are predominantly

Buddhist, and temples are in many urban and rural areas.

For decades, giving alms is a way of life for most Thais and a way of making merits. Thais depend on their respective monks in the learning, understanding, and practicing of Buddhism and during religious, celebratory, and funeral ceremonies.

In some other Buddhist places, monks and nuns are generally vegetarian. For Thai monks, any food given as alms should not be rejected, and thus they are expected to eat whatever is given.

Chinese Buddhist monks or nuns, who do not collect alms but cook their own food, have more control over what they could and should eat. Tibetan monks instead generally live in a harsh and cold mountainous climate and therefore do not have many vegetable staples in their meals. Hence, they are generally not vegetarian but do minimise meat consumption whenever possible.

Not having dinner is only practiced by Theravada monks, which are mostly in tropical climates. This too has practicality, as it may be not conducive in most cooler and harsher weather countries, for the body requires more energy and heat in daily activities under extreme conditions.

In Eastern and Buddhist philosophies, the emphasis has always been about eating the right way rather than about what we should eat. However, if possible, serious practitioners will avoid eating too much meat. Besides compassion towards all living beings, it is said that too much meat may make one more aggressive, such as what we see in carnivores, while herbivores are generally more gentle animals.

During his quest, Scott also discovered methods to reduce weight effectively and naturally. The antidepressants and heart medications had somehow increased Scott's appetite. He was putting on lots of weight and was heavier than he has ever been before, far from the athletic physique he once had. In Thailand, while temporarily staying in Buddhist temples, Scott was taught to eat slowly, to chew a lot, and meals were confined to breakfast and lunch only.

The famous Chinese quote to eat like a king for breakfast, prince for breakfast, and pauper for dinner is well known to most Chinese, but this is a step further.

To suppress or to fulfil hunger pangs during the long evenings and nights, Scott drank hot drinks and began to lose lots of weight daily. Within weeks, he was almost back to where he used to be and was feeling healthier too. He then studied about the practicality of eating slowly and for only two meals in a day. What he found out was astonishingly logical and wise.

Ancient Chinese teachings also advocate eating slowly and chewing a lot as a way of enjoying food more, reducing the amount one would normally eat, and benefitting the digestive system. Drinking hot drinks is a healthier way to substitute normal dinner whilst giving the stomach, which is one of the most utilised organs, a much-needed rest. Moderate eating also cultivates contentment and discipline.

Scott began to make these changes in his lifestyle, even until today, with an exception for special dinner occasions. His weight has remained almost the same, without any weight loss exercises or dieting programs for all these years. He focuses more on eating the right way than worrying constantly about what to eat.

Having experienced the luxury and comfort of the modern-day lifestyle with its regular gastronomic indulgence, Scott is now learning the benefits and pleasure of simple living and moderate eating. The comfort of a bed in a home or hotel could not provide the quality of sleep that comes from a peaceful mind, while the pleasure of food taken in abundance often resulted in the sufferings of indigestion or constipation.

Conventional modern life often advocates living life at its fullest, but ancient wisdom stresses on living it in simplicity. Scott could now experience the benefits to his physical and mental health during this simple lifestyle. In comparison to the consistent mental stresses in constantly trying to seek more comfort and pleasures of modern-day living, whether through an abundant lifestyle or the ever-insatiable greed for more, nothing ever seems to assuage those wants.

Living in luxury did provide Scott with more comfort and temporary pleasures, but it seemed hollow at most times. The experience of sleeping on a thin mattress on a cold bare floor and eating moderately provided him a more peaceful mindset as compared to the stresses of modern city life that often crept up unknowingly, despite the physical comfort.

His mental health improved significantly, which proved to have a positive impact on his physical health, just as what recent scientific findings had discovered and proven.

The patient's mental health is often his best physical healer, as most doctors would commonly say. In all these recent years, Scott's visitations to doctors due to sickness reduced tremendously, except on several occasions due to external infections, such as dengue or food poisoning. He was positive that his immune system had strengthened and that the cultivation of his mental health had also contributed positively to his physical health.

Strangely enough, there were not many ancient teachings concerning the development of health through rigorous exercises. In fact, subtle physical forms of exercises that were being advocated were by using the breath to connect the mind and body, such as yoga, tai chi, and qigong.

Ancient teachings focussed on the cultivation of mental health, which will also develop physical health, and but unfortunately not the other way around. Similarly to what we see in daily life, physically disabled people with a positive mindset seems to be able to live normally, while physically fit individuals with mental illnesses often can't – and in many cases choose death over living.

Modern exercise does have its benefits, but at times one may wonder if it is aesthetic charm or health benefits that takes precedent. In ancient teachings, mental health is being taught as crucial in the development of one's well-being, which inherently accentuates an aesthetic-enhancement as well as through endogenous bodily rebalancing. A smiling face from a peaceful mind is undoubtedly more pleasing to the eyes than an angry face from a disturbed mind. A person's facial expression can often be the reflection of his thoughts.

Scott eventually overcame his depression, but his doctor suggested he continue his medication for a few more years to prevent relapses. However, he has yet to recover fully and emotionally from the departure of his companion, whom he believed was the ideal one.

"Love is simply the wish for others to be happy" was a quote by a great Buddhist teacher. Love in the modern world or in movies has always been about romance, but in ancient teachings, it is completely different. This is what Scott learned from numerous old philosophy books.

Modern-day romances are typically based on these common lyrics or romantic movies lines we see and hear regularly:

1) I love you as long as you love me.
   This indicates conditional love, either when one loves in reciprocation or if one is being loved.
2) You belong to me and I belong to you.
   This indicates sense of ownership towards the other party. It's more a mental ownership rather than the ownership of a physical person during slavery times.
3) I can't live without you.
   This indicates the sense of dependency or portrays the depth of one's love. Unfortunately, it's also being used both a testament of one's emotions and threat at times.

In ancient teachings, the most altruistic love is said to be that of a mother for her child. *Love* is just simply the wish for the other to be happy unconditionally, in giving the loved one the freedom by letting go, which is, sadly, contrary to modern self-interpretation.

A mother's love is not subjected to being loved back, and regardless of what wrong her child has done, a loving mother would never cease to wish for her child to be happy, even at her expense.

A mother's love for her kids continue despite knowing well that they will leave her for education, work, or to start their own families someday. This does not prevent her from loving, as her wish for their happiness will take priority over her own happiness or the joy of having them beside her.

The letting go of their children for the sake of education, career, and matrimony, whether from a duration of several years, decades, or a lifetime, is all for the sake of their happiness. Their departure may cause a temporary void, a feeling of separation, but it does not stop a mother from living out a life of her own.

In old teachings, love is not subject to conditions, ownership or dependency but is to hope for the other to be happy, regardless of whether they are together or not. It's often said that loving the right way will either reduce or prevent the pain of separation and undoubtedly avoid the often-seen transformation of one's love into anger and hatred during breakups and divorces.

These were the first few of the numerous profound teachings Scott discovered throughout the next few years in his quest to find ancient solutions for modern problems.

These teachings helped Scott transform his resentment towards his former companion, for leaving him when he was in most desperate times, into compassion towards her. Everyone wants to seek happiness and to avoid sufferings as what is being taught by existing wise monks. In fact, in years to come, and until this very day, Scott never ceased to extend his ex-companion the annual birthday and Christmas greetings, with well wishes for her new companionship and their eventual matrimony.

Scott often has anger, hatred, or regret all within a single day, occasionally lasting for days. These ancient wisdoms helped to transform Scott's mental and emotional roller coaster into one that is calmer and clearer.

These ancient wisdoms were instrumental in Scott's mental and emotional change towards his companion that had left him earlier. The hurt and pain were transformed to acceptance and letting go, both contributing greatly to a more peaceful mindset.

This also enhanced further his pursuit to find answers for his existing heart problems, to prevent future blockages and the development of other heart illnesses.

Scott also travelled to Tibetan settlements and monasteries in Northern India and Nepal to pursue further his quest to learn and practice more about ancient wisdom in self-cultivation and answers to modern-day problems.

From wise ancients' wisdom teachings, Scott is now to able to see for himself how many wise, young, and old Tibetans were living out their lives based on these very foundations. Their resilience towards the hardship of living in poverty does not compromise their pursuit of continued learning and putting into practice what they have learned in daily living.

What amazed Scott while watching Tibetans living in North India and Nepal was their mental strength. It was both difficult and harsh living in a foreign land as refugees for decades, but this did not seem to deter them from smiling regularly and being friendly.

From them, Scott discovered that heart attacks and strokes were uncommon within their communities; and Alzheimer's, Parkinson's and dementia illness were as rare as the heart diseases. The two most common illnesses there are diabetes and dysentery sickness caused by too much sugar content, possibly due to the influence of Indian's sweet tooth culture and unhygienic water or food.

Scott's biggest problem was heart and mental illness, and in these settlements, these were the least problems. *What is it that the Tibetan have done to avoid these illnesses which are so common and are the biggest killers in many countries?* Scott often asked himself.

From various discussion and observations, what Scott found out is that the Tibetans seem to focus on the cultivation of mental health far more than physical health, contrary with most city dwellers. Not only was this apparent here but also in Thailand. Scott noticed the same principle from the teachings of Buddhist monks about the importance of mental health. Developing mental health is regarded as more important than physical health, as the former can cultivate the latter – but not in reverse.

One Tibetan monk was even heard to have said, "It's OK if my body is sick, as long as my mind is not sick." This also resonates to why most who commit suicide are physically healthy people, while those who are terminally ill often recover, especially amongst positive minded patients.

During the past few years, Scott had been very disciplined in learning and practicing meditation to tame and calm his mind to prevent another relapse of depression, which would be very dangerous for him. Scott began to research more while practicing more extensively his daily meditation to develop and sustain his mental health further.

Another year passed, and Scott was personally convinced that a healthy mind is also a healthy heart. With that in mind, Scott would soon embark on one of his most dangerous life-threatening decisions after several years of intensive studies and practices.

Scott visited his heart doctor for his regular checkup. The results were impressive. Existing minor blockages in non-crucial arteries were either reducing or cleared, no new blockages were found, and his heart was functioning normally. These were the deciding factors for Scott to make a life-threatening decision.

Scott told his doctor that he would stop taking all his heart medication immediately, just as he has done with his antidepressants. His doctor was stunned and repeatedly advised him against it. He also told Scott that by doing so, chances of his having a heart problem would be extremely high and possibly fatal within six months.

The years of putting into practice all that he had learned about the cultivation of mental health had cleared all remaining blocked arteries and lowered his blood pressure and cholesterol level.

Through extensive and deeper research into ancient Eastern wisdoms, Scott was sure that the cultivation of his mental health through meditation would contribute to the development of a healthier heart.

For Scott, taking such a drastic and dangerous decision to stop all medications was the only way he could fully convince himself of the correlation between his mind and heart, just as how the Eastern languages have referred to them in oneness.

To his doctor's advice, Scott responded, "If I were to die by then, please forget all I have told you about meditation and the oneness of the heart and mind."

Meditation had now become his only way to prevent relapses of depression and heart problems, but all these have yet to be thoroughly researched or proven scientifically at this point of time. Scott had to dig further into ancient teachings, as his life was at stake now. The more he read and practiced, the more convinced Scott was about the cultivation of mental health and its correlation to physical health.

The mind was not only Scott's source of mental and physical illnesses in the past but was also the cause of his daily mental vexations when things didn't go his way, in dealing with roller coaster emotions, and controlling his temperament in tense situations.

"We are our worst enemies"; "To conquer others is strong; to conquer ourselves is mighty"; and "What we think, we become" were some of the foundations derived from old teachings that contributed to Scott's realisation of the importance of taming and calming the mind.

For most Asians, prevention has always been far more important than cure, as they demonstrate in their daily lives. Coconut and certain teas are cooling drinks during hot seasons to prevent internal heat from accumulating and causing illnesses. Medicinal herbs are taken when one is still healthy to develop a stronger body to prevent falling sick.

As for Scott, with his Chinese background and mindset, despite being Western educated for all of his academic life, meditation as a way of prevention for his mental and heart illness and future relapses makes perfect sense.

The success of losing weight in such a short period as part of his accidental discovery during his learning journey widened his quest to find more solutions to daily modern city living problems for all ages.

Eating two meals a day is indirectly fasting or giving the stomach a rest. Various health benefits in fasting have been proven by modern science, and the stomach is probably one of the few most overworked organs. In Chinese teachings, the stomach is said to be the main cause of many diseases, while in Buddhist teachings, it's said to be the dirtiest part of a human's body, consisting of faeces, urine, and undigested food. As such, moderate eating is the natural way to manage weight and sustain health.

Eating moderately also helps in promoting self-discipline, perseverance, and endurance, which are essential for self-cultivation.

The purpose of this is to advocate good health that can allow an individual to not only prolong health but also assist in achieving mental tranquillity.

Food are often being taken not only to fill the stomach but occasionally to overcome boredom, as a distraction in dealing with unpleasant circumstances, or to fulfil the desires which are being aroused by *ophthalmoception* (sense of sight), *audioception* (sense of hearing); *gustaoception* (sense of taste); *olfacoception* (sense of smell); and *tactioception* (sense of touch). In fact, most will even eat simply by just thinking of food.

In Buddhist philosophy, the mind is construed as the sixth sense; in addition to the physical sensory senses of modern science. It teaches about the five sensory senses and the sixth being the mind, all with its own consciousness.

Scott eventually moved back to be with his family but still sleeping in his own room, as in the past. His children had now grown up to be young adults and experienced their own pressures in education and their social lives. Fortunately, they excelled in their studies and studied in top schools. Scott's mental health is now excellent and his annual heart checkup shows no abnormalities.

He then was offered a new job working with former business counterpart and friends as colleagues. It was a friendly and cooperative environment, and Scott was posted to Indonesia. Scott was back to his healthy self again, but then complacency crept in. He began to fall back on his learning and practice, thinking that all that he had learned and practiced was sufficient for the rest of his life.

His new company was a multinational company filled with many ambitious personalities, but Scott could perform his contractual obligation and expand it beyond his scope of responsibility.

After several years, new management were put in place and most of Scott's closest friends were either transferred or left the company. It seemed history was beginning to repeat itself.

At the same time, Scott's mother had fallen ill and was extremely weak. He and his mother had been very close and kept in contact daily for years through phone calls. Not much was spoken during these phone calls, but he knew they would mean a lot to her. Scott did not want to repeat the mistake he had made for not spending enough time with his father when he fell ill.

He travelled back to be with his mother as much as possible, but her health deteriorated further. She died a year later, after just managing to celebrate the Chinese New Year with all her children. They were all devastated, for it was a close-knit family.

As years passed, Scott subsequently had to report to a new superior that was just being posted over. He was highly ambitious, dominating, and listened to no one but himself, in complete contrast to the one that had hired him.

Scott's lack of practice in both meditation and self-cultivation was apparent in his inability to control his nemesis's temperament. Discussions turned into arguments, and subsequently both parties decided mutually to terminate the existing employment contract, which had a few more months before its expiry.

It was a relief for Scott to retire finally from the corporate world after almost three decades, even though he was only fifty. But the sadness over the demise of Scott's beloved mother often overwhelmed him. Scott and his siblings decided to venture into elderly home care, as they understood the difficulties of taking care of ageing and sick parents for those who must juggle between careers and/or young families.

It was a social venture not designed to make huge profit but one that would serve as a remembrance for their late parents and as part of putting to practice what Scott had learned about compassion.

While it may not be profitable, Scott found it to be enriching spending time there with the tenants.

Most of the tenants were suffering from dementia or Alzheimer's disease, with several of them completely bedridden. These issues further strengthened Scott's determination to find the prevention to these mental illnesses, which are becoming more apparent in recent times.

Financially, Scott had enough to retire comfortably and to pursue other interests. During the first year of his retirement, Scott was finding difficulty in filling up his time with activities. The boredom soon aroused his discontentment. With that, negativity about life and future years ahead again started to affect him emotionally.

While he still had significant amounts of funds, his greed to acquire more began to grow, and soon his attachment to what he already had affected him each time he had to pay bills.

This turned into anxiety about the future and exaggerated nonexistent problems into uncontrollable fears. His greed for more and deep attachment to what he already had caused him to try to protect all that he owned from reducing.

This mentality, with lack of practices in controlling his mind, caused Scott to again fall into another depressive mode. Scott was fortunate to have a supportive family, siblings, and a couple of genuine friends to count on, but again, only he could pull himself out of this.

His lack of practice was mainly due to the ignorance that all these years of meditation would have been sufficient for the rest of his life, not knowing that the ancient teachings taught that these practices are to be lifelong, for as long as we are alive. Thoughts will come and go, thus the need for one to understand constantly the causes of phenomena.

Most have briefly experienced the state of meditative mind without even realising it. For example, when we look at the beauty of a sunrise or sunset, many will just be experiencing the momentarily calmness while enjoying its beauty. Some renowned meditation masters have more appropriately described the meditative mind as the gap when we are in between thoughts, with meditation being a means to extend this gap knowingly and widen it to experience deeper calmness and peace.

We can all relate to the fact that from the time we wake up in the morning and until we sleep, our minds are filled with one thought after another, even while dreaming while sleeping. It was said that even if we were to hide ourselves in a cave, we couldn't escape from a busy mind and that no family or friends can do a greater good or harm than our own misdirected minds.

Scott's latest depression proved to be the most severe; he knew the effects of meditation and tried desperately to overcome it himself.

His former psychiatrist's comment rang through his head regularly. Would he suffer from schizophrenia or commit suicide this time?

He went for long walks to clear his mind and get some exercise, as many would have advised. All these provided temporary relief, but soon all the negativities were back in his mind. Scott desperately tried to meditate but was unable to do so, for the thoughts of worries, anxiety, sadness, and fear were running wild uncontrollably.

Scott's family were affected mentally and emotionally. They had been supportive but soon were trying to stay away from him. He knew that they were being dragged down by his mental and emotional state. Scott had to get away from them for their sake.

He had siblings living in Kuala Lumpur, and he went there to get away from his family. It was not an easy decision for him, as being away from them was the last thing on his mind. He spent several weeks at his brother's home in KL, hoping to wake up from this nightmare.

His supportive siblings provided him with all the assurances and comfort he needed, but none seemed to have a lasting effect. He travelled to Thailand to meet with some friends, hoping that their companionship would give him more strength to overcome it. Being with them was comforting, but when Scott was on his own, he could not tame his wandering mind.

He had no choice but to seek medical treatment again, as suicidal thoughts began to surface in his mind daily. The medication made him drowsy, as in the past, but it helped him sleep, which was the only time he could be temporarily eased. Again, side effects began to kick in; he could not stop eating and was in the habit of taking an extra dosage to keep him mentally numb longer.

He knew the causes of his problem and ways to overcome it, but preventing is easier than curing the illnesses that occur, just as the saying that prevention is better than cure. Scott had to go back to the basics on ancient teachings and with the help of a spiritual teacher, who subsequently convinced Scott to write a book about his life experiences.

The feelings were all too familiar: worrying about the future, exaggerating existing problems into uncontrollable self-imagined disasters, anxieties turning into fear, and negativity in almost everything.

Many have partially experienced these emotions for a short duration and overcome it. For one to be regarded as having fallen into a depression, these emotions would have had to last or continue for several weeks.

Many often ignore the state of depression as a temporary emotional setback. In contrary, a person in depression will either have a prolonged depressive mood, unable to snap out of it, and often will have suicidal thoughts.

Depression often comes with similar symptoms but the severity is being measured by the intensity of the negativities of one's mind and its effects on individual daily lives, such as socialising, eating, and sleeping.

In Buddhist teachings, it is said that as long as greed, hatred, and ignorance persist, anyone will face the risk of mental and emotional sufferings. These are said to be the causes and are deemed as the three poisons.

Scott knew of these profound truths, but he was unable to thoroughly put the contentment into practice and not worry about the future, as with most city cosmopolitan dwellers. The greed for more and worry about losing what he already had was the direct result of these relapses.

The only truly effective way to prevent this is for one to learn to control his thoughts through meditation, for it's the uncontrollable mind that needs to be controlled.

There are many temporary reliefs, such as exercising, taking a walk in nature, listening to music, or being in the company of good people. But as with alcohol, sex, and drugs, these provide mere temporary relief, although without similar terrible after effects.

Despite all the ancient wisdom that Scott had learned and practiced over the years, greed, desire, and cravings had again taken precedence over contentment. The effects of not practicing meditation to calm the mind for the last couple of years were also taking their toll. Despite all the good he knew about meditation, he was in no position to put any of it into practice, as he was overwhelmed by negative emotions from his present uncontrollable mind.

Each time negative thoughts arise, one of the effective ways to subdue them is to be in the present by just being aware of the breath and not following the thoughts further. With this, it will often just vanish and the mind will be diverted with a new "job", to just be aware of the breath instead of wandering off with the thoughts.

A Buddhist saying is that we should guard our minds as closely as one should guard the thatched roof to prevent rainwater from seeping in. It is the reminder of the need to regularly practice in taming and controlling one's mind for life.

For Scott, it was back to the elementary school of life. He tried for several months to avoid modern medication, thinking that he could overcome it with his knowledge and determination. But as many wise sages have advised, theories without practice do nobody any good.

Scott had failed repeatedly to get back on his own feet, and after realising that he had fallen back into depression, he knew that he needed the temporary assistance of modern medication to assist in maintaining enough mental stability for him to cultivate his mental health again.

The usual advice to anyone suffering from depression is the notion to think positively or to be strong. However, in reality, despite these truths, there are more immediate baby steps that need to be taken before one can generate positive thinking and be mentally strong again. For Scott, while the antidepressants might subdue the constant negativity in his mind, once the temporary chemical relief was over, he had to deal with it on his own.

Distraction, cutting out negative thoughts, developing positive thoughts, and then learning to control the mind are the steps needed to overcome depression.

To distract his mind, Scott spent his time watching numerous movies until he grew tired and fell asleep. This worked, as he was no longer sinking deeper into depression. Scott decided then to taper down his medication, as he feared that addiction was forming from the constant habit of taking more doses than recommended by his doctor.

From the distraction next came the task of stopping the negative thoughts each time they occurred. To achieve this, Scott focused on his breaths each time his mind began to think negatively. At times, this could last for hours, but it was more comforting than living with constant anxiety and fear.

Soon he began to read again and meditate like a crippled learning to walk again. This rerun episode of his depression reminded him of the destructive nature of the mind if left uncontrolled, but he had also learnt how constructive it can be when it's calm and clear. Scott must begin taking the baby steps again.

Scott's continued pursuit in learning and practicing had changed his temperament into one that was more calm and controlled. Realising now that everything is subject to change and nothing is permanent, as ancient's teachings have stressed, he could let go of the attachment for money. Accepting all things and letting go of unpleasant ones were now part of his new life mantra instead of trying to blame others and holding on to anger as he used to do.

He finally stopped his medication after tapering it off for a couple of months when he no longer depended on it to sleep or to calm his mind. Scott eventually recovered from his latest depression after a long eight months of battle.

Scott continues to travel again to various part of Asia, including India, China, and Thailand to learn more about ancient Eastern philosophy and practicing meditation. His kids had excelled in their examinations, and both were awarded prestigious scholarships to further their education in Ivy Leagues and top local universities. This provided Scott the opportunities to travel more and longer without having to take care of or worry about their tertiary education.

Thailand was where Scott had spent the most time learning meditation and where he had his first experience of temporary monastic living. For him, it offered the most conducive environment, for his quest and familiarity with the country provided him the most convenient destination in the revision and expanding his knowledge into Buddhist philosophies.

For centuries, India and Nepal have been the melting pot of various religious pursuits, besides being the birthplace of many ancients philosophical teachings, with an ancient renowned education centre such as Nalanda (currently being rebuilt and functioning after being destroyed during the Ottoman Empire). The close resemblance in Indian and Buddhist philosophies offer conducive comparative studies of philosophical teachings.

Taiwan and China is the appropriate place to seek ancient Chinese wisdoms and to observe how they are being practiced and preserved in several holistic places. Being a Chinese man, ancient Chinese teachings were also a way for Scott to understand more of his own culture, which ecologically offered more familiarity.

Chinese teachings offer broad overview particularly on mental health. It also focuses on the nature and bases its teachings from there. Most of its teachings are concentrated on causes and effects. However, to go into the details of cultivating mental health, Buddhist teachings are more profound.

As with Scott's other travels, no prior planning was done as he travelled from one country to another. He was living each day at a time and trying to be in the present as much as he could. Not having any expectation as to wherever he was going prevented him from being disappointed, as it is said that disappointments arise when expectations are not met, just as with the ancient saying that a good traveller enjoys every bit that comes by along the journey and is not tied up with plans or schedules.

Without any travelling companion for months, Scott began to learn to enjoy the solitude without being lonely. To him, this was perhaps the real freedom, the ability to enjoy being with oneself for any period, something Scott had never been able to do in the past.

Good companions are vital during travelling, for we are all social animals. However, in situations where an equally or more knowledgeable companionship is lacking, it is then taught that it would be better for one to roam alone like an elephant in the forest.

What Scott learned with interest was spirituality without religiosity. These ancient's teachings are not dogmatic, offer no salvation, and are non-theistic. It's all about learning to understand, practicing to experience, and having self-cultivation in handling and overcoming problems. In brief, it's about acquiring knowledge through reasoning, gaining wisdom from understanding, and practicing to experience.

As a definition, spirituality is a broad concept, with room for many perspectives. In general, it includes a sense of connection to something bigger than we are, and it typically involves a search for meaning in life. As such, it is a universal human experience that touches us all.

In contrast, religions offer hope in times of desperation and are centred around salvation and dogma and are highly based on faith.

Despite being a religious person when young, Scott was determined to explore an alternative way instead of being fully dependant on a creator in dealing with his problems.

Ancient philosophies not only explain in detail the causes and effects of phenomena but also teach ways to handle and overcome problems. Its similarity with multiple religions is in the aspects of virtuous living, love, and compassion.

To study the numerous old Eastern teachings requires lots of time and efforts. It always advocates the discipline in the learning and practice while encouraging an open mind to analyse with deep contemplation in order to comprehend its teachings fully. For Scott, these gruelling criteria were worth undertaking for the sake of his mental health and well-being.

A profound Buddhist quote that no one saves us but ourselves, that we ourselves must walk the path, serves as a reminder to Scott's self-reliance since moving to Singapore almost three decades ago.

Similarly, Scott constantly tried to teach his children since when they were young to depend on themselves rather than to be dependent on others when facing life's predicaments. It was now time for Scott to practice what he had preached. Unpleasant past experiences resulting from dependency on others, both in his search for happiness and in overcoming problems, had been nasty reminders of self-reliance.

Accepting what had happened and letting go are often easier said than done. However, with wisdom on impermanence of all things and understanding that holding on to the past does nobody any good and it's a waste of time will help one put this into practice.

Being dependent on others for long-term happiness in the past had turned out desperately painful when things went awry. Being alone but not feeling lonely gave Scott his first experience of self-emotional dependence and his first taste of holistic freedom.

However, he also realised that no man is an island, and during his travels, Scott met many people from all over the world, developing friendships with some while sharing what he had learned along the way – but never imposing his views.

Amongst the many valuable lessons Scott had learned over these years is that good things should not be selfishly kept. As the old saying teaches, "Good things we should share."

On his way, back from his travel, Scott went back to his hometown, Taiping, in West Malaysia. Taiping is literally translated as "everlasting peace" in Chinese. It is also the wettest town in Peninsular Malaysia, with an average rainfall of four thousand millimetres per year, twice the average of the country, and it is also known as the "Raintown".

Situated in the north, Peninsula Malaysia it is surrounded by hills, lush rainforests, and a beautiful lake in the middle of the town – a paradise of natural beauty for nature and peace lovers. Scott parents' home was centrally located but had a beautiful natural forest behind it.

From his room's balcony, he viewed a beautiful and natural self-grown rainforest with its own residents of monkeys, birds, snakes, and even a family of wild boar. To Scott, it was like living in a forest but with modern amenities as the same time. It then became and still is Scott's favourite place for self-retreat and meditation.

Years ago, Scott would have been bored to death staying in a big home by himself for just a couple of days and, like most, would constantly occupy himself with activities, socialising, and eating. However, he has now learnt to enjoy being in solitude, but that does not stop him from meeting old friends or making new ones.

His days start at 5.00 a.m. for meditation, before heading out for breakfast at 7.00 a.m. at the popular local eateries that had been around since Scott was a teenager. From there, Scott mainly spends most of his time in the hills, forests, and streams that are situated at the edge of the town.

Life is simple here, but more importantly, it's extremely peaceful, living up to its name Taiping, or Everlasting Peace. Taipingnites, as many would call its residents, seem to have a better quality of life than what Scott had seen in big urban cities, despite being financially poorer. The locals are not only contented with what they have but are charitable, despite not being rich, much like what Scott had seen in Thailand, Bhutan, and Tibetan settlements in North India.

From his travels, Scott learned that the simple way in gauging the politeness of people in this part of the world was by the frequency of cars or motorbikes blasting their horns. Here one could hardly hear that. To him, this reflects tolerance and patience, and it makes him proud of his fellow Taipingnites.

Evening rain is the norm here; the afternoon sun will evaporate the morning dew and condense into clouds. With hills surrounding this town, rain clouds will regularly form, creating rain as they climb higher. For many, it's a relief from occasional afternoon heat, while providing a natural soothing sound therapy for the evenings.

Scott never failed to visit a small orphanage in the town, and the kids were always excited about seeing him. For them, it will mean a good meal outside, going for a swim in a natural public pool, or watching movies.

What Scott had learned from old teachings is that the best way to be happy is to make others happy. This theory proves itself each time he is with the kids, and it has convinced him of the practicality of old wisdom in daily life as well as an old Tibetan saying that good clothes we should wear; good food we should share.

Simple living has its benefits, and living on needs instead of wants does not require much. The wants are what have gotten many into trouble, turned into burden that never could be fully satisfied. Scott had now realised that most of the expensive things he owned were not what he had needed but merely the wants that brought only temporary pleasure. Seeking happiness externally, whether it's through things, food, or people, is not lasting or sustainable. Happiness is an inside job, and it became Scott's mission after he discovered the wisdoms of the ancients, who had been advocating this for centuries.

What he thinks each day affects what he feels and thus affects what he says or do. The quality of each new day for Scott depends on the quality of his mind, just as an old Tibetan saying: "Whether you feel warm or not depends on the sun, whether you feel happy or not depends on the mind."

For Scott, guarding his mind to avoid it straying into greed, hatred, and all the negativity was far more important than constantly trying to fill it with things to do, places to be, and people to be with.

Happiness, as it had been taught by some ancient sage, was just having peace of mind.

While this term is often being used widely during both ancient and modern times, few have managed to experience it over a long period. A state of equanimity can be achieved when the mind is stable and not easily aroused or disturbed in times of excitement or difficulties. By living in the present, not dwelling on the past or worrying about the future, peace of mind can be sustained over a longer period.

Meditation is described as the penetration beyond the waves of thoughts into the calmness beneath the sea or through the clouds of thoughts into the clear open sky.

A peaceful mindset will often provide one the internal strength in dealing with life's predicament, as an old Chinese quote states: "When the mind is at peace, big problems becomes small; when it's disturbed, small problems becomes big."

With these profound truths, Scott no longer seeks to fill his days with activities or people but does not abstain from it either. With this mindset, he somehow just let the days go by on their own. If anyone contacts him, he would make the effort to be with that person; otherwise, he would either spend his time with nature or read to acquire additional ancient wisdoms.

To Scott, this was also the realisation of self-dependency and solitude; all that was needed was a calm and peaceful mind. In the past, while he may be lying in a tranquil five-star beach hotel with all its amenities, his mind was constantly wandering all over, thinking about work or worrying about problems that had yet to arise. Despite all the physical comfort, relaxation and peace are not to be found in a busy mind.

This quest will continue, as learning is a lifelong process and problems are part of life. However, most of them are merely the creation of an untamed mind, and in many cases, they do not materialise. For those that do, what Scott learned is that if there is anything that can be done to solve a problem, do it; otherwise, there isn't any point in worrying about it, as that will not solve anything.

By simply changing the perception of one's mind, emotions can be thoroughly transformed. For Scott, nothing was now more important than cultivating and maintaining a mind of equanimity, which is one that does not get too excited or affected in good and bad situations, for all things are subject to changes and are impermanent.

A friend of his once told him that she preferred nightmares than sweet dreams because she felt relieved waking up from a bad dream but often saddened from waking up from a good one. For Scott, life situations are sometimes no more than just a dream.

This mental stability has also proved to be benefitting his physical health. Despite not taking any medication now due to his previous heart problems, Scott does not seem to fear any further recurrences or even death. It was like a new lease on life instead, far from the old one for him, which had his mind controlling his life.

Being an active person, Scott realises that all physical abilities have limitation as he grows older, but gaining knowledge and the development of mental health are limitless, just as the ancients have taught. In fact, it's more like a good wine that gets better as it ages; however, unlike wine, it does not get better, being static, but requires a lifelong continuous process of learning and practicing.

Ancient philosophies are based on logic and knowing the intrinsic of nature and mind. It advocates for it's teachings to be reasoned out, analysed, and tested rather than believing by faith. For Scott, who had always been inquisitive, this itself resonated well with him, as pragmatism had always been his way of life.

Chinese and Buddhist philosophies' survival over the centuries and continued influence in the lives of many all over the world is a testament of everlasting wisdom. These ancient teachings have always been based on the intrinsic state of nature, and its wisdom is both simplistic and profound. Furthermore, its practicality and effectiveness are easily tested and experienced.

Confucius, China's greatest thinker and philosopher, was quoted as saying, "I am not one who was born in the possession of knowledge; I am one who is fond of antiquity, and earnest in seeking it there."

Unlike knowledge, which comes in many forms, it is also said that knowledge is the skill we learn to make a living. Wisdom is the skill of living.

While Scott may have acquired much ancient wisdom in over a decade through reading numerous books, putting it into practice is a different story, for theories without practice did not improve his life. Furthermore, it's only through practicing that he could experience and test the effectiveness of these profound teachings.

The quest will continue with passion and learning. For Scott, nothing seems to be greater than the pursuit of one's well-being and the experience of having a more peaceful and meaningful life. To share without imposing, learn to understand, study with reasoning, and practice in order to gain experience will be a continuous quest in his journey of spirituality without religiosity.

Made in the USA
Columbia, SC
02 December 2017